PASSION FOR THE PIECE

Cyndi Sibley

Sibley Press
Contact: passionforthepiece@gmail.com

Scripture from www.biblegateway.com.
Library of Congress Control Number: 2016905340

All the stories in this book are true. Actual names of the people involved have been changed to protect their privacy.

Thank you, God, for enlightening me to enlighten others.

I was born and raised Catholic and that is the religion I practice today. I respect all religions and am intrigued by many. I didn't choose to write this book to preach what I believe is the right way. "God" can be taken in this book any way you want to imagine. God may be light, energy, or an image of a human being. It is whatever you choose to believe. I chose to write this book to share our family's journey with autism and how the importance of faith and gratitude stands above all.

CONTENTS

PASSION FOR THE PIECE

FOREWORD

I was born and raised in a suburb of Detroit, Michigan. Anyone who knows me personally knows that I tell it like it is—straight from the heart. People or critics shouldn't have to question why. I'm from the Motor City, a stand up and tell it like it is city.

When our daughter was diagnosed with autism fifteen years ago, "standing up and telling it like it is" was difficult and keeping it real is still the hardest part. For all the times I would rather run and hide or just live in denial, it's faith that keeps me afloat when I feel as though I'm drowning.

This isn't a book with all the answers or a book that reveals the missing piece to the devastating puzzle that is autism. This is just a book about my life, autism, and everything in between.

1

THE PLAN

Trust in the Lord with all your heart, and do not lean on your own understanding. In all your ways acknowledge him, and he will make straight your paths.

—Proverbs 3:5

The air was heavy after a late afternoon rain. I glanced down at the wet grass as I walked across the park. The voices of parents and fans yelling and cheering echoed in the humid air behind me. I kept turning around to keep track of how the baseball game was going. As I walked farther away, the voices softened and my feet seemed to be sinking into the thick, damp grass. The world around me began to close in and suddenly there was silence and darkness.

Where am I? Where is everyone? Where are my children, my husband? Do they know where I am? What if I'm dead? This can't be it! I'm not finished with my life. My children need me!

Suddenly, like a movie, the memories I cherished from my childhood till the present played in my mind. I began to watch my long, auburn hair blowing in the wind as my mom held my hand and walked me to school on that first day of kindergarten.

I was back in time. I could feel the warm September sun beating down on my head as I inhaled the scent of flowers from our neighbor's garden. I was happy and carefree. Only laughter consumed me, as I watched my friends and myself standing barefoot on the street corner at our lemonade stand. Next door to us was the neighborhood clubhouse where we spent our days. It was filled with old trunks that were filled to the top with costumes from past dance recitals. This was where we held our weekly talent shows for the neighborhood kids.

As these memories unraveled, and kindergarten faded to adolescence, I began to see my life unfolding before me. Suddenly my past shifted to the present and there before me were my husband, my children, and my home. In the distance I could hear the soft music of a harp playing. It was peaceful and relaxing and I could feel myself becoming drowsy. When I looked around

I was surrounded by white. It was a dense fog and I could hardly see anything in front of me. My feet felt like they were walking on clouds and it seemed as if I were floating. I could hear faint voices around me. I tried to follow the sounds of the voices to lead me to where they were coming from.

I could hear somebody asking, "Is it you? Will it be you?"

I wasn't sure if this person was talking to me, so I asked: "Are you talking to me?" The voice said, "Yes, you. Will it be you?" I really wasn't sure what this voice was asking of me, but I replied, "Yes, it will be me."

The harp that played in the distance became louder. It was becoming less peaceful and more annoying. Suddenly, my eyes opened and there next to me on my nightstand sat my cell phone with the harp ringtone of my alarm blaring. I took a deep breath and thanked God that it was only a dream—although I believe this dream delivered a meaningful sign as to the purpose of my life.

2

LIFE'S PURPOSE

Then your light will break forth like the dawn and your healing will quickly appear, then your righteousness will go before you, and the glory of the Lord will be your right guard.

—Isaiah 58:8

How is one's purpose in life determined? I don't think a person's purpose is based on how much money they will make, how many good times and memories they share, or the power and fame they achieve in society. I feel that one's purpose is to be the good in this world and to be an example of our maker, whether it be in a career as a doctor or firefighter that helps people, as a parent who provides unconditional love, or as a blind person who teaches us to appreciate sight.

What leads us to the path of our purpose? Is it destiny or do we have the freedom to choose? I believe my purpose in life was to be a wife and mother. It's a satisfying feeling in my heart that confirms what I am doing is right, despite any challenges I may face. At the end of those most challenging days is when I really feel like I accomplished something.

I think everyone has to have a purpose; otherwise, life would seem worthless. Maybe that's why some people consume themselves in drugs and/or alcohol, because they haven't found their purpose. Everyone is always striving for something more or something better and they don't stop to see the good that they already have.

If there was a job posting that read, "Seeking person to be mother of child with autism" and listed the job requirements, I don't think there would be a line of people applying. In fact, most people would run in the opposite direction.

Instead, everyone would be standing in line for the job posting that was easy, fun, and exciting. If this is true, then why do those people who have everything still feel empty and unsatisfied? I believe it's because people need a purpose to find fulfillment.

I have always had a need to help people. There are a few experiences over the years that had a significant impact on my life. I often relate these experiences with my life's purpose today.

When I was in grade school, our special education classes were isolated from the rest of the school. Special education students seemed to be hidden at the far end of the building; rarely would we see these students during recess. This was in the mid to late '70s and "no child left behind" was pretty much unheard of.

During recess one day, a boy who was mentally challenged and severely obese was looking for someone to interact with him. On these days when the special education classroom students joined us during recess, he would chase me all over the playground. It was starting to make me feel uncomfortable so I would run and hide when I saw him coming. Finally, one day I said hello and he asked me to push him on the merry-go-round. He then asked me my name and I told him. He wore a smile from ear to ear for the remainder of recess. This made me think how a little act of kindness can go so far. After that day, we spent most of our days interacting at recess. I relate this experience to the compassion I feel for children with special needs.

When I was in sixth grade my friends and I decided to hold a fair in my backyard to raise money for the Jerry Lewis Telethon. We made up games and sold popcorn and lemonade to raise money. I can't recall how much money we raised, but I do remember how excited I was to deliver the money to one of the telethon locations. This fundraiser opened my heart to the joy of giving.

When I was about six months pregnant, I was outside on a sunny day sanding a rocking cradle that I had found at a thrift store. I planned to refinish it and use it in our firstborn's nursery. I heard footsteps behind me and when I looked there was a girl in a wheelchair with her mom pushing her. They lived about two doors down from us. The girl was severely handicapped and the house that they lived in was always shut up and never showed any sign of activity going on. It bothered me that the house always looked so dark and depressing. I was happy that day to finally see them outdoors enjoying the beautiful weather. As I continued to sand the cradle, I thought to myself, "I hope I never become so depressed not to enjoy life whatever the circumstances may be." This memory reminds me to keep a positive outlook and to not drown in pity.

I was about eight months pregnant with our daughter Jackie when I attended mass on Ash Wednesday, which is a day of fasting and the first day of Lent in the Catholic religion. When I kneeled down to pray, I remember looking up at Jesus on the crucifix at the front of the church and asking him to bless my child and to protect him or her from the world around us. I was asking for protection from all the evil and corruption in our world. That day is still so vivid because I often think of Jackie and those affected by a disability and how they remain so innocent.

All of these experiences often cross my mind. I think of them as seeds planted within me to grow and fulfill my life's purpose.

3

FOR BETTER OR FOR WORSE

Therefore what God has joined together, let not man separate.

—Matthew 19:6

If you were to ask me back when I was seven years old what I was going to be when I grew up, my answer would have been, "I'm going to get married, have seven children, and live on a farm." I always dreamed of getting married and having a family.

It was during my twenties that I noticed an ad in our local paper advertising a search for dancers to audition for Disney World. I had studied dance since the age of six and have always loved it. I thought this would be an exciting opportunity. Regardless if I made the audition or not, I was ready to make a move. I packed up all my belongings, moved to Florida, and got an apartment. On the day of the audition there were over 600 people auditioning and they were looking for 10 dancers. Unfortunately, I did not make the audition, but I continued to live in Florida and worked in a law firm for the next couple of years. As much as I enjoyed the beautiful weather, I missed my family and friends terribly. I ended up moving back to Michigan and applying at my previous place of employment, where I was hired back.

Thinking back, I had the freedom to do what I wanted, when I wanted, with no questions asked. I liked it that way, free and in control. However, as I got settled into my thirties, the thoughts of marriage surfaced again, and having children was now questionable.

"For better or for worse." Do people really take this literally? Because when life is good, love is great! It's during those times of trials, heartaches, and disappointments when true love is tested. Today, when the going gets tough everyone wants a ticket to Easy Street. It does seem inviting to just detour off the road of construction and away from the roadblocks and head down Easy Street, free from hassles and aggravation.

During the first years of our relationship we were on Easy Street; better yet, I think it was more like the Highway to Heaven. Dual incomes, vacations, night life, and plenty of good times. Life didn't seem like it could get any better.

My husband and I have always had a great relationship. We are similar to yin and yang. Chinese philosophy explains how yin and yang are opposite or contrary forces which are actually complementary, interconnected, and interdependent in the natural world. If you've ever read the book *Men Are from Mars, Women Are from Venus*, you have an understanding of the differences between men and women. Men just want to fix the problem and move on. Women want to embrace the problem, talk about it, and explore all different ways of solving the problem.

My husband, Chris, is a realist. He has always been calm and reserved when it comes to emotions. I, on the other hand, am a dreamer who wears all thoughts and emotions on my sleeve. He thinks concrete, usually with a plan in place, and I like to go with the flow. Punctuality is top on his list and on the middle of mine.

When Chris and I first met it was before I had moved to Florida. I thought he was attractive, but nothing ever came of it. It was years later before our paths crossed again at Chris's brother's wedding. This time, I wasn't going to let him get away. Yes, there were fireworks and I knew in my heart he was the one. I had no doubt that this was the man I planned to spend the rest of my life with. Shortly after two years, we were married.

We purchased our first home two months after we were married. Just a few months later, we decided to make our house a home and start a family. Starting a family wasn't an easy decision for us in the beginning. We were both in our thirties and worried that we had become too set in our ways. It was a conversation I had with my grandfather that changed my outlook on family and made us think otherwise.

My grandfather had asked the question one evening about when we were going to start a family. I told him we weren't sure if we were going to have children.

"What do you mean? No children? That's what's wrong in today's world!" he shouted. He was shocked that I would consider missing out on starting a family. I did entertain the thought of children, but I was afraid of change. Starting a family would change my whole life. I just couldn't imagine it. I felt it was too late and that I had missed the opportunity years ago when I was younger.

My grandfather was old-school and stood for strong values. My grandfather and grandmother started their family when they were very young, which was common in those days. My grandfather went off to war and my grandmother moved in with my grandfather's parents while raising the first few of their eight children. My grandfather kept the family grounded and worked hard every day to provide. He was a loving husband and wonderful father. He loved life and had an unforgettable laugh that was contagious. He made the best "pickled anything," ranging from cucumbers and beets to cauliflower and eggs. His rhubarb jelly was always a family favorite too. He rode his bike all over the neighborhood well into his eighties and relaxed each day on their front porch. He knew almost every person that passed down his street. I looked up to my grandfather and witnessed his great example of parenthood.

Our decision to start a family wasn't based solely on my grandpa's opinion, but it did make me step back and really examine his life and all the blessings that come with children.

4

THE BEGINNING

Children are a gift from the Lord, they are a reward from him.

—Psalm 127:3

When I was pregnant with our first child I felt wonderful, probably better than not pregnant. When I was just past my due date, the doctor suggested that I get admitted into the hospital and they induce labor the following morning.

After hours of labor and an unsuccessful attempt by vacuum, a C-section was performed. The baby was lodged in my pelvic bone area; the doctors had to tug and pull the baby back up through the birth canal to deliver her.

"A baby girl," the doctor announced shortly after midnight on March 11, 1999. The APGAR score was perfect and we counted ten fingers and ten toes, a healthy 8lb. 2oz. baby girl. We were thrilled! When the doctor brought her over to me, he commented on how long her fingers were and that she would someday make a great pianist. We named her Jacklyn Nicole. She had jet black hair that was about two inches long and stood straight up on the top of her head.

Within a couple of days, I was sent home to begin full responsibility as a new mom. As a secretary in the workforce, I could multitask and I was always up for any challenge, but I have to admit I was scared to take on this new position. My husband was back to work the next day, so I was on my own.

I've been told that motherly instincts come naturally, but she was so tiny and I felt so clueless. Initially, things went smooth. I was nursing every two to four hours, changing diapers, burping, rocking, etc. Jackie was jaundiced so we had a special light she had to be put under to treat her. Every couple of days, my mom and I made a trip to the hospital to have Jackie's blood checked until she was no longer jaundiced. After a few weeks the crying pattern set in.

It was every evening just around dinner time that the screaming would start for hours. It gradually became worse and the crying continued throughout the day. It seemed endless. We switched formulas, added cereal to her bottle, and tried every remedy imaginable for colic.

Finally, the doctor suggested that we take her for an upper gastrointestinal x-ray. To perform the x-ray they needed to wrap Jackie with a blanket tightly around a board. As she screamed, I stood helpless beside her and watched.

The results of the x-ray revealed that she had a reflux problem. The doctor suggested adding more cereal to her formula so that it was thicker, which would help her digest better. There was no improvement and with all the cereal she was eating she was rapidly gaining weight. After a couple of months, the colic was gone. It wasn't long after things finally quieted down that I was pregnant again.

My second pregnancy seems like a blur when I think back to how busy I was with already having a toddler. It was much different during my first pregnancy when I could take naps and really embrace each stage of my pregnancy. This time things seemed to be moving much faster.

Further into my pregnancy a routine screening was done to detect neural tube defects and Down syndrome. This test tends to deliver high false-positives. So when the results of the test showed up positive we tried not to become too alarmed. The doctor suggested an amniocentesis be done for more accurate results. Chris and I decided that no further testing be done because no matter what the results were, we were having this child.

Labor and delivery went much smoother the second time around. I was admitted into the hospital so they could induce labor. Within a few hours after I was induced, I delivered our 8lb. 1½oz. healthy baby boy. Thank you, Jesus! We decided to name our beautiful son "Cole," which means "People's Victory" and/or "Conqueror."

We couldn't wait to get home and introduce Jackie to her new baby brother. When we arrived home anxiously awaiting Jackie's response, there was nothing. It was almost as though Cole was invisible.

5

A CRACK IN MY WORLD

In the day when I cried out, you answered me, and made me bold with strength in my soul.

—Psalm 138:3

Spring 2001, I arrived at Jackie's pediatrician's office. Jackie was due for her two-year well visit. We met with her pediatrician and the normal routine took place. During the exam, the doctor started to ask questions regarding her developmental milestones.

"Does she speak? Approximately how many words can she say?" With hesitation in my voice, I said that I didn't recall her speaking much lately, but I did recall her first words of "mama" and "Elmo."

"Does she interact with other children?" the doctor continued.

"She played with her cousins at her first birthday party and over the holidays, but she hasn't been around other kids much," I said.

"Does she respond when you call her name?" the doctor asked.

"Sometimes? Well, that's if she's not watching her Baby Mozart video," I answered. The doctor suggested having her hearing checked just to be on the safe side.

I left the office that day happy the exam was over with little concern about the hearing test. When I arrived home later that evening, I decided to Google "symptoms of hearing loss" and up popped the word "autism." Autism was a word I only associated with the movie *Rain Man*, starring Dustin Hoffman. When the symptoms of autism filled my screen, I found myself checking off nearly every symptom. In denial, I deeply tucked away my thoughts and shut down my computer. Chris was expected home soon so I headed upstairs.

Chris arrived home and as soon as he stepped foot in the front door I blurted, "We need to talk!"

I began to tell him how the exam at the pediatrician's office went and that the doctor requested to have Jackie's hearing tested. Then the word autism came up and tears started streaming down my face. I shared all the symptoms that fit Jackie.

"Don't believe everything that's out there. They can make anything seem like that. I wouldn't worry till after the hearing test," he said. We both glanced over to where Jackie was sitting. She was glued to the television as she watched her favorite Baby Mozart video. I suggested that Chris throw his keys on the ground to see if Jackie turned around or noticed. Chris then dropped his keys on the hardwood floors behind Jackie. They made a loud clunk but nothing happened. Again, he threw his keys and still no reaction. Trying to convince myself, I turned to Chris and said, "You know how she loves this video, she isn't interested in anything else right now." Chris reassured me that night that everything was going to be all right. I nodded in agreement, but I wasn't convinced because somehow a mom just knows.

I began to think that a slight hearing loss didn't seem so bad. We could always get her a hearing aid. Anything was better than the haunting word of autism. I took Jackie for her hearing test appointment and the technician called back that afternoon to report everything was normal. I was relieved but at the same time disappointed.

The results of the hearing test were forwarded to Jackie's pediatrician. Within a couple of days, I received a call from the pediatrician suggesting that I call the county school district for an evaluation.

Her in-home evaluation was scheduled for March 12, 2001, the day after her second birthday. Jackie's second birthday took place at our home with her grandparents, aunts, uncles, and cousins. Things were much different at this birthday compared to her first birthday. On her first birthday, we shared it with family and friends, plus a special appearance by Elmo. The party was recorded on video and she seemed very interested in her surroundings by the way she was interacting with her cousins. She played with her cake and ate it with her hands.

On the day of her second birthday party, Jackie sat in her highchair, disconnected and staring off into space. She seemed distant and her face was hollow. There were no changes in her expression and no interest in opening gifts, eating cake, or playing with her cousins. As much as we all tried to play with her and share in the excitement, there was still no response. Our little girl was gone, vanished from us and locked away in a world of her own.

Looking back, all the signs seemed clear, but then I had every excuse imaginable. She's tired, she's overwhelmed with so many people, maybe she doesn't feel well, and the list went on. That day I knew in my gut there was something terribly wrong. The party ended and after everyone left that evening there was still no mention of the "A" word.

The next morning I planned to meet with someone from the school district to conduct an evaluation on Jackie. Hopefully, we would know more, something simple that we could fix…I prayed.

MY LITTLE COCOON

Your journey into this world was quite challenging that day;
I remember how I prayed that everything would be OK.
God answered my prayer when I saw you before me;
Ten fingers, ten toes, a healthy baby.
The nurses showed me how to fold your blanket at night;
they explained to fold up from the bottom, then fold to the left, then right.
I followed their instructions right to a tee;
you wrapped in a cocoon there before me.
This vision still remains so clear in my mind;
you nestled in this cocoon who I'm searching to find.
I want to crawl into that cocoon with you;
to experience the things you do.
Your cocoon will one day transform you into a butterfly;
and like an eagle soar above us near the heavens so high.

6
EARTH ANGELS

Do not neglect to show hospitality to strangers, for thereby some entertained angels unawares.

—Hebrews 13:2

I believe there are angels put here on earth to help those in need. I'm sure of it because I have been blessed with many.

When Jackie was two years old, the day after her second birthday, we had the county's school district come to our home and do an evaluation on her. That day was as clear as yesterday. Ms. Smith arrived at our home and greeted me with a warm smile. She was tall and carried herself with confidence. She resembled the actress Blythe Danner. She was dressed casually and carried a large tote bag along with her binder and purse. She was very friendly, which helped to ease the anxiety I was feeling. We decided to conduct the evaluation in our living room, so we sat down together on our living room floor. Jackie was wandering close by and was busy keeping herself occupied by checking out her surroundings.

Ms. Smith began to pull out of her bag wooden blocks, bubbles, and toys. Ms. Smith's eyes were glued on Jackie to carefully watch and observe to see if there was a response to any of the items she was pulling out of her bag. Jackie was oblivious, and showed no interest in either of us. I then turned up the volume on the television to draw her attention to the Baby Mozart video that played. "This will do the trick," I said. I was sure that Jackie would turn around and engage with her favorite video playing. This was our "rescue video" that we turned on during times when Jackie needed to calm. I shouted, "Jackie, Baby Mozart is on!" Still, no response.

We explored different ways to get Jackie's attention, but we had no success. The more Ms. Smith called out to Jackie, sang songs, and blew bubbles, the further away she seemed. It was as though we were invisible. Ms. Smith recorded data during the different activities and attempts to interact with Jackie. It was similar to a teacher correcting a test you knew you completely failed. Things were definitely not going in the direction I had hoped for.

Ms. Smith gathered her belongings and said she would be in touch soon. When I asked her how Jackie did, she said she would have to look things over and get back to me. I thanked her for coming and walked her to the front door. As I closed the door behind her, my mind raced out of control with worry.

The next day Ms. Smith called to schedule an appointment with their school district's psychiatrist to do another evaluation with Jackie. Our conversation was brief with still many unanswered questions in my head.

Chris and I attended the evaluation and watched as the psychiatrist tested Jackie on various activities. She asked Jackie questions and worked on getting her to imitate simple commands. We observed Jackie stacking blocks one by one making a very tall tower. We were impressed and thought, she can't be autistic, look at how coordinated she is. We couldn't stack a tower that tall if we both tried! Neither my husband nor I had any idea if she was passing this test or not. It was hard to know if Jackie was demonstrating the expected behaviors of a two-year-old.

The evaluation ended and they met with us to go over their observation and the results. Their diagnosis was autism. We both listened and controlled all the emotions that were swallowing us up. At the end of the meeting, we shook hands, said thank you, and left the building.

As we drove home, I stared out the passenger's side window and the world around me appeared lifeless. Tears were running down my face. I could not talk and could hardly breathe. Every inhale and exhale was as though I were grasping for air. I felt paralyzed. How was I going to go on? I can't do this! I can't!!! Little did I know, Ms. Smith would soon be my angel in disguise.

The following week I received a follow-up call from the Autistic Impaired Program through the county school district. They informed us that early intervention was key so they suggested we begin the program as soon as possible.

When we arrived the first day we were welcomed by a team of smiling faces filled with optimism and determination. Ms. Smith was the lady in charge and she ran the program. Tall, strong, and on a mission was how Ms. Smith carried herself. She was on a mission to get these parents informed and prepared for their journey ahead.

Every morning I would load up my double stroller and head to class with Jackie, who was two years old, and our son, Cole, who was about six months. After we arrived, we would check the visual calendar schedule. Everything was labeled with a word and picture.

Flashcards were used constantly. We would sing songs and pop bubbles to promote eye contact and visual tracking. We also worked on following schedules and transitioning from one activity to the next. The program also taught us strategies on dealing with meltdowns and calming techniques; support was also given to the parents who would occasionally have their own meltdowns. This place was a Godsend.

There were about six families in the program. We all became close as we shared our stories and our tears. I became especially close to another mom who had a son the same age as Cole. Both of us arrived every day with our double strollers. As we focused on working with our children in the program, our six-month-old boys played together. It was heartwarming to see the two interacting and playing together. This mom and I became friends and also attended a conference together to see Temple Grandin, an autism activist and consultant to the livestock industry on animal behavior. This conference was a wealth of knowledge regarding autism.

Ms. Smith always knew when to give you that boost of encouragement just when you wanted to give up. She would set us straight when we blamed the autism on ourselves, such as eating tuna while pregnant or not spreading the vaccines apart. When the kids would throw themselves to the ground and scream, bang their heads, kick, and bite, she would push up her sleeves and stand firm and tell us not to give in to these actions. She often reminded us, "You have to work on getting these behaviors under control because it becomes really out of control when they're older." We all had so much respect for her and held on to her every word as though she was a great scientist performing an experiment.

Ms. Smith would make visits twice a week to our home. She would show us activities to work on and help us put together calendars, schedules, and booklets to promote communication. She built my confidence and gave me the tools to believe that things were going to get better. This earth angel scooped me up under her wings and prepared me for the journey ahead.

Other angels who have touched my life are teachers. When I refer to teachers I am referring to teachers, social workers, speech pathologists, and occupational therapists. A good teacher wants to make a difference in your child's life. We have been blessed with extraordinary teachers that have gone above and beyond. During all the different phases and stages of Jackie's life, they have stuck it out and tackled all the problems that came along. They have searched for solutions and given me a hug, if not physically, then emotionally. These teachers have made a difference. I am so grateful for all of their support in our lives.

7
UNTAINTED SOULS

And we know that all things work together for the good to those who love God, to those who are called according to his purpose.

—*Romans 8:28*

Does God look down from above with a tear in his eye? Is his heart broken by the devastation and disease brought into this world? Was it man who started most problems which could have been avoided? Bombarding infants and toddlers with vaccines at such a young age, adding chemicals to our food and land, are just a few to mention.

Autism is a disease that hits home for me because I believe it robbed our daughter's ability to enjoy the fullness of life. Not just our daughter, but many children. I don't believe that you are born with autism. I believe autism happens when your body is so bombarded with toxins that the immune system can't withstand the battle it's up against, whether it be thimerasal (a chemical used as a preservative in vaccines), pesticides, or other chemicals in our air, land, and food. These chemicals destroy the body, creating a symptom (sensory malfunction, poor eye contact, delayed speech, lack of social interaction). When too many symptoms surface, the diagnosis is most likely autism. Today, we lack nutrients in our food and our systems are depleted. Too many vaccines are given, especially at such a young age. Those most affected are children with weakened immune systems. Let me stress that I am not opposed to *clean vaccines* given on a *safe schedule*.

I was undecided about the title of this chapter. I couldn't decide between "Tainted" or "Untainted" Souls. "Tainted" is regarding the causes of autism.

"Untainted" is regarding the pure innocence that radiates through the souls of those affected by autism. "Untainted" was more appealing so I went with that.

Jackie loves music and she has great rhythm. She sang before she could talk and occasionally I am lucky to hear her sing a song in its entirety. Jackie was five or six years old when she began to speak, only a few words, but she could sing entire nursery rhymes and songs. When she sings, she lights up a room. Jackie can be affectionate, but for years I could barely get a hug without sending her senses into overload so today I take whatever I can get. She has a strong intuition that's accurate. You can't fool her. If you are a mean person she will pick up on it. She knows a fake! Same goes for people who are intimidated by her or fearful; she will use this tool to manipulate you and get her way. Just because a child may not speak does not mean they are stupid or can't hear. These children are very bright so never underestimate them.

WHY?

Beautiful children born each day in this world we know today;
then between the ages of two and three they suddenly slip away.
The doctor across the desk says your child has autism, I'm sorry;
and tell you there's no cure, insurance won't cover it, and there's material at the library.
You educate yourself and try to learn all about it;
you even rent Rain Man to imagine the torment.
Everyone is giving you advice on what you should do;
it's like hitting the lotto and being taken as some fool.
One thing is certain that we know for sure;
there's still not enough research for a cure.
We need to explore and move ahead;
point us in the right direction so we're not misled.
What's happening to these children is a puzzle no one can understand;
some say it's mercury in the vaccines, preservatives in the food, chemicals in our land.
Instead of hiding and denying it,
all we ask is they start resolving it.
These children are our future, don't they see;
who will fight for our land of the free?

8

OUR PIONEERS

For he will command his angels concerning you to guard you in all your ways.

—Psalm 91:11

A majority of the people who work with individuals with special needs are certainly not doing it for the paycheck. Their passion to help people is what points them to this profession. Great teachers and caregivers go beyond their forty-hour week. They believe in the goals that others may find unrealistic. These people give families encouragement.

After Jackie was diagnosed, the county we were living in at the time suggested that I apply for a Medicaid Waiver (Medicaid is a state program that provides in-home services for individuals with disabilities). This waiver provides respite care and services such as occupational therapy and speech. Occupational therapy and speech were rarely covered by insurance in 2003, so having the waiver was a huge asset.

The waiting list for a waiver is long, but it was worth applying since it was based on the needs of each family. My husband was traveling and working most weekends.

Shortly after applying, I received a call from my county caseworker informing me that a waiver may be available. She explained that I would have to fill out an application and be interviewed prior to their consideration for approval of the waiver. The interview was very extensive with every question imaginable. The following week, I received a call from my caseworker informing me that the waiver had been approved and granted. This was great news! The next step would be to find staff whom I could trust with Jackie.

The county started sending to our home applicants for me to interview. A majority of them I wouldn't have hired to watch our dog. When you are out of breath just climbing our basement stairs, I highly doubt they are going to catch a four-year-old who frequently elopes!! I was feeling pretty discouraged; I was yet to see a "Mary Poppins." My caseworker called one evening while I was finishing dinner dishes. I remember it clearly. She said she had a lady about my age who had experience with a girl with autism who was a couple of years older than Jackie. She was available to come that evening for an interview.

The woman arrived about a half hour later and seemed experienced and straightforward. I really appreciate a person who's honest. She was married and had one daughter. She struck me as enthusiastic and confident. She loved animals, especially dogs, and seemed to like our four-month-old puppy. I decided to give her a shot. Kay started the following week. She came into our home that first week and took care of business. When I was probably at my most vulnerable state, she gave me the confidence and hope that everything was going to be okay. Each day after she arrived, I would usually venture out for a jog around our subdivision. I still wasn't ready to leave too far from our home. After a few weeks, she suggested that my husband and I go to dinner one evening. She reassured me that she would call if she needed anything. With hesitation, I let my guard down and trusted her suggestion. My husband and I went to dinner. It was wonderful! It was almost as though we were dating again. We were able to eat our dinner in peace and catch up with one another. After that night, it became a weekly thing and Thursdays became our date night. Kay ran a tight ship in our home, always enforcing schedules and rules. She seemed to genuinely love and care for Jackie. Kay helped me to gain the courage to venture out which helped keep our marriage alive and gave me time away to recharge my batteries. After a couple of years, Kay was busy with the responsibilities of her own family. Her hours were starting to decrease, so I started looking for an additional staff person.

The county had assigned me a new caseworker. This caseworker was very nice and suggested a girl to work with Jackie. When she left for college, she referred me to a friend of hers who was also wonderful. Karen was soft-spoken and loved to read. She had a calmness about her that was pleasant opposed to my often chaotic world. Jackie took a liking to Karen. Karen stayed with our family for several years. She had a friend who was home from Michigan State for the summer that was looking for employment. I was interested and had her come for an interview. I hired her on the spot. I liked Kayla the minute I met her. She was a natural with children. She sparkled with positive energy. She had four siblings and her experience around siblings and being brought up in a large family showed as she interacted with Jackie. Although she had no experience with autism, she was fun, loving, and Jackie really enjoyed her company. Kayla always took such pride in Jackie. She always made sure her hair was combed and worked on teaching Jackie good manners. Kayla quickly became a part of our family. She worked us into her schedule with school and would come home on weekends or breaks. My husband and I were able to take weekend trips to get away. We always felt secure knowing Jackie was in safe hands with Kayla. Kayla continued her employment with our family through all of her college years and ended up pursuing a career in special education with her endorsement in autism. She still keeps a relationship with our family and Jackie. Jackie developed such a bond with Kayla over the years that it's difficult when Jackie doesn't see her as often. Understanding separation is difficult for most children on the spectrum. Over the years, Kayla has been a blessing to our family. I know in my heart that she will go places in serving individuals with special needs. I believe this is her passion.

I continued my search after Kay, Karen, and Kayla slowly faded out of our lives. One morning as I was putting Jackie on the bus for school, I approached the bus aide about potential staff. She quickly responded that she would definitely be interested in working with Jackie. This aide, Brielle, was a beam of sunshine! Every morning and afternoon when I saw her she always had a smile on her face. It didn't matter what kind of day she was having, she would always say that Jackie did a great job. I even remember an incident when Jackie had an upset on the bus and went to pull Brielle's hair, without realizing it was a hair extension piece. Jackie's meltdown stopped in midstream when the aide's entire wig pulled off her head. Jackie was shocked to see how much hair she pulled out, which quickly redirected her out of the upset. Brielle, on the other hand, was humiliated since this was all recorded on the bus camera. We still laugh about it to this day. Shortly after Brielle started with our family, she ended her position with the transportation department. Jackie loved being around Brielle. Brielle accompanied our family on a vacation to Disney World. She fit right in with everyone and was such a great help to our family. We were ready to move her into our home, but as fate would have it she fell in love, got married, and moved to California to start a family of her own. That was a rough time for Jackie and all of us to see her go. It's been so hard to try and explain to Jackie that she's gone after building such a close bond with someone. Brielle still faithfully visits Jackie each time she comes home to Michigan to visit her family. We keep in touch through email with pictures and updates.

Monique is another person who worked with our family and has known Jackie the longest. They met when Jackie was in kindergarten. The school that both Monique and Jackie attended offered a mentor program where the older general education students helped out in the autistic impaired classroom by interacting with the students. Monique was drawn to Jackie and began to build a relationship with Jackie right away. She came to visit the classroom throughout their years in elementary. When we moved out of that school district, Monique moved on to junior high and high school. Jackie and Monique drifted apart, but we still occasionally kept in touch. When Monique was in her last years of high school, I decided to hire her to help out with Jackie.

Monique genuinely loves Jackie and I feel like they have a good friendship because they are so close in age. I would venture to say that Jackie see Monique as the one friend whom she associates with school. Monique also comes from a large family and has always been so nurturing with Jackie. Monique has the drive and has always been active in student council and is a great advocate who promoted autism awareness at her high school. Monique was willing to accompany me on a road trip to Disney. She was a great support. I really couldn't have done it without her. Her navigating skills from Michigan to Florida and being a hopper with the fast passes at Disney was a tremendous help. Monique is currently going to college and will still visit Jackie during breaks.

There were also other staff that have floated in and out of our home over the years. Many were wonderful for short periods, soon realizing they just couldn't do it, while others worked to fill the gap over summer vacations. I have always kept my feelers out to look for potential staff, since they are so difficult to find. I think times are becoming more difficult as Jackie continues to grow and the meltdowns become more intense. People are intimidated. It is one thing to have a four-year-old kicking and screaming during a meltdown; it's quite another to deal with a sixteen-year-old at 175 pounds during a meltdown.

9

"SORRY, BUT SHE'S TOO AUTISTIC"

Do not judge, or you too will be judged. For in the same way you judge others, you will be judged, and with the measure you use, it will be measured to you.

—Matthew 7:1-2

S*orry, But She's Too Autistic* is what my husband wanted me to name this book. "I'm sorry" are the too often familiar words we hear when Jackie is not accepted at camps or programs because of her level of autism. It amazes me the number of individuals who want all the glory, but yet have no guts to deal with the behaviors that accompany the moderate to severe degrees of autism. They want to be viewed as helpful and compassionate people in the autism community; however, they have little tolerance for the challenging side of autism. Most of the camps I've experienced prefer individuals on the higher functioning end of the spectrum.

"All the glory, but no guts." "When the going gets tough, bail!" This doesn't sound like a caring, compassionate camp run by directors with years of training and knowledge in autism, does it?

In May 2013, I received information about a summer camp held outdoors. I thought it would be nice to explore this option since the summer camp she had been attending was held indoors. This outdoor camp offered activities such as swimming, horseback riding, and ziplining. Jackie loves the outdoors so I thought this would be a good fit. I called and spoke with a lady who answered questions. She suggested that I schedule an appointment with their director to come to our home and conduct an interview and meet Jackie. On the day of the appointment, the director and her assistant arrived in a black Hummer. I invited them into our kitchen, where the evaluation took place. She asked questions and I filled her in on Jackie's behaviors and the triggers that can lead to aggression. She assured me that they were well aware of and experienced with these types of behaviors. They seemed confident to handle anything that came their way. I stressed the importance of doing social stories and schedules. I also explained that waiting was very difficult for Jackie. She smiled in a condescending way and again reassured me. During our evaluation, I think more attention was focused on the expenses of the camp and when the deposit would be due. I introduced Jackie to them and neither of them seemed curious to learn about Jackie's interests, likes, or dislikes.

The first day of camp, we arrived on time. It was about a forty-five-minute drive from our home to the camp. I introduced myself to the camp counselor and gave them a few last-minute instructions. That first day, all I could think about was how Jackie was adjusting. I could hardly wait to pick her up and find out how her day went. When I arrived for pickup, the counselor said she had a good day. I was relieved with the news, but still wished Jackie was able to communicate this to me. When I asked her how her day went, she said, "Good." "Good" was usually her response no matter if it was a good day or a bad day.

We arrived ready to begin the second day of the camp. I was feeling less anxious and more confident that this could be a good experience for Jackie. I didn't receive a call from the camp so I assumed another successful day. When I arrived at the end of the day to pick up Jackie, the director who initially met with me was staring as I pulled in. There was also a guy who was her assistant standing next to Jackie, his eyes also glued on my car. *Oh no!* I thought. My stomach knotted up.

I stepped out of the car with a smile on my face and hoped for good news. Before I could even say hello, the director's assistant met me shaking his head back and forth, saying, "It was not a good day at all." The director, who was standing close by, didn't even make eye contact with me. The assistant said that the director would be calling me that evening. I took Jackie by the hand and left. As we drove home I looked in the rear-view mirror and asked Jackie how her day was. "Good," she replied. I couldn't shut off my mind. All the way home I thought about what might have happened. I called Jackie's middle school teacher and asked if the camp director could contact her. I thought it would be helpful to brainstorm some strategies to whatever problems they needed to address.

I received the director's phone call that evening and was shocked at what she told me. Apparently, the counselors decided to take the campers down to the lake for swimming. When the campers reached the lake where they were going to swim, they were told that the campers were going to have to wait because there were still other campers changing into their bathing suits. *Waiting?!* I thought. That was trigger number one. When I asked, "How long did she have to wait?" she said, "No more then ten minutes." *Ten minutes is like an eternity to most children on the spectrum,* I thought to myself. "Did you do a social story explaining that she had to wait first, then swimming?" "Nope!" she replied. She then proceeded to tell me that Jackie threw herself to the ground and started screaming and becoming aggressive. She also added that it took three people to physically move her during the upset, which resulted in her biting one of our counselors. The director finally finished with, "Then she pissed herself!"

First of all, this director obviously didn't listen when I said waiting was difficult, social stories work great, and don't try to move her during a meltdown. Plus, what kind of cold-hearted individual uses the words "pissed herself"? My daughter doesn't urinate on herself. This was an indicator that she must have been pretty traumatized with the situation and how they went about handling it. My blood was boiling as I continued listening to both the director and her assistant director hash out all the details on speakerphone. I tried to defend Jackie with the triggers that caused her to react in this manner, but I felt I was getting nowhere. I suggested that they call her teacher so that they could have a plan in place going forward to help make things successful. Reluctantly, the director agreed to contact Jackie's teacher that evening. Later that evening when I spoke with Jackie's teacher, she said that the director kept cutting her off and would not allow her to make suggestions. She felt that their phone conversation was a waste of time.

The next day when I dropped off Jackie I tried really hard to be cordial, but it was difficult. *I will be surprised if she makes it through the day without a phone call home,* I thought. All day I couldn't stop thinking about Jackie. Later that day, when I arrived to pick up Jackie the director's assistant was sitting on the sidewalk with Jackie. Jackie looked calm and content. I walked up to the director's assistant and asked how her day went. He replied, "Not good, we are very sorry but she won't be able to continue with our camp." "Can I ask what happened?" I asked. He said, "She was anxiously pacing to go on the water slide and then when it was her turn she did not want to get out of the water. She would not follow directions and this posed a problem for the other campers. I'm sorry, I just don't think it's going to work out." Was I hearing things? Was this a joke! I couldn't believe what was going on. They were throwing my daughter out of camp for this? The director, who again was just walking distance away, never even made an attempt to come over and explain. I took Jackie by the hand and Jackie turned to the director's assistant and said, "See you tomorrow." I said, "No, not tomorrow, Jackie, we're not invited back!" We got into the car and as I cried on the drive home I thought, *I don't want her at a place like this anyway.* But unfortunately, all the camps in our area were already filled for the summer. This was going to be a long summer ahead with no structure, camps, or staff to help out.

I had received a flyer during the spring of 2013 regarding a new camp in the area. The flyer indicated that it was an overnight camp that was being offered to children ages nine through sixteen with autism. At first I couldn't even imagine sending her anywhere overnight, but I was curious. I thought this might be good for Jackie to try something overnight and away from home. I contacted her teacher to get her input and she said it sounded great but she didn't know much about it. I asked if any other parents inquired or were considering sending their child. I would feel much more comfortable if Jackie had a peer from school going. There were parents interested; however, nobody had made a commitment. I decided to contact the camp the next day. I spoke with the director of that camp for about an hour. She tried to convince our family to give this a try. She felt it would be great for Jackie, plus our family would benefit with some respite. I explained that I was fearful how Jackie would do being away from me since she had only stayed with her grandparents. The camp would provide separate cabins for those children who were sensitive to noise, non-sleepers, etc. I asked what they would do if she was to get up in the middle of the night. She said there would always be someone awake at all times and that they would make sure Jackie was as comfortable as possible. I requested an aide to work one-on-one with Jackie since re-direction may be needed, sensory breaks, and a close eye on her for fear of elopement. She said they would be happy to accommodate those needs and that they would love to have Jackie attend their camp. She reassured me that they were very experienced and that Jackie would be in good hands. Before hanging up, I said I would need to think about it and talk it over with my husband. I contemplated the thought of her going somewhere, especially overnight. The what-ifs in my head went on and on… "What if they don't understand her needs or wants? What if she has a horrible time and hates me for it? What if she escapes out of the cabin at night?" *It would probably be easier to just say no, I thought to myself.*

Everyone I consulted with, including Chris, my mom, Jackie's teacher, and friends all told me that it would be good for Jackie and that I could really use the break. I did imagine how nice it would be to have five days free to do what I wanted. No bedtime rituals, no meltdowns, we could have friends over… Maybe we should just try it, I thought. I called the director of the camp back and said that we were going to send Jackie. The camp application that needed to be filled out was long and very detailed. Questions ranged from what Jackie likes to eat to triggers that upset her and what strategies work best. This camp was willing to hear what I had to say. I thought that this camp finally got it. As the week of camp drew closer, we rehearsed social stories with Jackie and reviewed the calendar of the days ahead. I wrote social stories on all the exciting activities they offered such as horseback riding, ziplining, and swimming. Jackie seemed excited and started to look forward to going. Seeing her excitement made me feel more at ease.

The morning arrived and it was time to pack up the car and take Jackie to camp. I was a nervous wreck, but held it together and focused on the positive. I kept telling myself that the separation would be good for the both of us. When I arrived at the camp, there was a welcoming committee that greeted us. Everyone was very accommodating. They kept talking to Jackie. "Hi, Jackie, do you like bubbles? We have bubbles or arts and crafts, which would you like to do, Jackie?" I was already thinking...too many questions! I could see that Jackie was already overwhelmed. *Remain calm, it's going to be okay,* I continued telling myself. The camp counselor said, "Mom, we got it from here, you're all set to go now." "Oh, okay", I said. Although quite honestly, I was hoping I could have volunteered at the camp that week. I kissed my sweet girl goodbye and asked her guardian angels to keep a close eye on her. The camp did not allow phone calls the entire week. The counselor would call the first night to let us know things were settled in, but after that there was no communication.

When I arrived home, I didn't know what to do with myself. It seems when I get that taste of freedom, I'm lost. Later that afternoon, I received a call from the camp director letting me know Jackie was fine and that she settled into the camp. She said she would call if there were any problems. That night it was a quiet night at home. It was actually nice to relax and watch TV with my husband and Cole. This is something I rarely do since I'm usually with Jackie. It was about 10 o'clock that evening when I noticed a text on my phone. It was from the camp director asking if there were any bedtime routines they may be forgetting.

They were having trouble with Jackie going to bed and she was very upset and crying. I called her back and explained that I usually read books before bed and stayed in the room until she fell asleep. She said that the counselor did read a story, but then it's lights out and all campers were told it was time for bed. She apologized and said they were not allowed to lie on the bed with the campers because of camp rules. I understood. I would be uncomfortable with the camp if they did allow this. Could they sit in a chair and just reassure her that they were there with her? I thought. This was her first time away from home and her routine. I tried to convince myself into thinking that this was all very new and that the first night away would probably be difficult. I asked that the director call me back or text me to let me know when she fell asleep. It was an hour later that another text came through saying, "Please call, Jackie is very upset!" When I called her back, she asked what they could do to help calm her since she was still very upset and disrupting the other campers. I suggested that they take a flashlight and let her walk outside. Taking walks usually helps to redirect Jackie and the flashlight at night might help to get her mind refocused. It was torture waiting for the next text or call to find out the update. *Is this even worth it?* I wondered. *She is probably traumatized and will probably hate me for this since I was the one who convinced her of how much fun camp would be.* It was after midnight when I finally received a text saying, "Rough night! She finally fell asleep." Before going to sleep that night I prayed that God would watch over her.

The next night came and we had planned on having friends over. Cole was able to invite a few of his friends to swim and have pizza for the night. That evening I was getting texted about the same time with the same situation, only worse. Jackie's behaviors had become aggressive to staff and herself. They actually considered me picking her up that evening. I told them if she didn't settle down in the next hour, I would be there to get her. I wanted more than anything to race over to the camp and take her home, but I also wanted her to achieve the goal of getting through the night successfully. I thought, *If Jackie figures out that aggressive behavior equals mom comes to the rescue, this will be trouble in the future.* I tried my best not to show my emotions in front of our guests. This was the one night Cole was able to have his friends over. About an hour later camp texted and said Jackie finally fell asleep. The next morning the camp director called and said they would try one more evening, but if there was a problem I would have to come get her. That evening I received another text. My heart was racing and I was ready to go pick her up. The text read, "Good night, Jackie is asleep." *Hooray!* I thought. I was so proud of this accomplishment; I knew how hard it was for Jackie.

The morning finally came for me to pick Jackie up from camp and I couldn't wait. When I got there, it wasn't the warm welcome I was expecting. It was almost to say, "Good riddance!" I saw Jackie across the room and her face was serious, with no smile. *Uh-oh,* I thought, *will she hate me for this?* One of the counselors greeted me and was very sweet. She gave Jackie a big hug and said she would see her next year. When I saw the camp director, I thanked her again for everything. She replied, "Boy, she was a rough one!" in a joking way, but she got her point across. We said our goodbyes and left. That was Jackie's last year at that camp. The following year they informed me that Jackie would not be accepted.

Both of these experiences were stressful and disappointing to our family, especially Jackie. It is an example of how these children with the most challenging behaviors often fall by the wayside.

Thankfully, there is a center in our area on which I can rely that accepts individuals on all ends of the spectrum. Jackie has attended their summer camp over the years and has also been involved in programs that offer socialization, cooking, and activities for children and young adults on the spectrum. The people who work at this center are experienced. They have always dealt with any challenges in a positive and constructive manner. This center has been a blessing to families.

10

ALTERNATIVE APPROACHES

Ask, and it will be given to you; seek, and you will find; knock, and it will be opened to you.

—*Matthew 7:7*

There are many different interventions that have helped children with autism. We have tried many. I think every parent should try every form of therapy their guts lead them to. As a parent, you know what's best for your child—don't forget it! First and foremost, you need to back the approach 100 percent. If you don't have a positive attitude to try a new approach, your child will sense it and you won't have the drive to succeed. Jackie has always been very intuitive with my feelings. If I'm nervous or agitated, she knows it.

Before we began our first intervention, blood work was needed. It was difficult for me to watch as Jackie was being poked and probed day after day while blood tests were being conducted. I had to lie across my four-year-old, pinning her down while they drew vials of blood for testing. I couldn't help but feel doubtful if this approach was really necessary. Was this going to cure her? I didn't know at the time what or if anything was going to help. I did know that blood tests were crucial to find out what avenues we would take as far as where she was deficient and what supplements would need to be added to her diet. Let's face it—parents are desperate for anything that can possibly help their child. If there was a glimpse of hope for anything, I was going to try it.

My "Supermom" cape was wrapped around my shoulders as I headed out to explore every intervention imaginable. Below is a list of all the interventions/therapies we explored and a brief description, my views, and the results for each one.

- 4 month ABA program at center - age 5
- Occupational Therapy-Sensory Integration - age 2 - still ongoing
- Gluten/Casein Free diet - age 3-8
- D.A.N. (Defeat Against Autism Now) Doctor - age 4-8

- Supplement Program (vitamins & minerals) - age 4-present
- Glutathione Intravenously - age 4-6
- A.I.T. (Auditory Integration Training) Therapy - age 7
- Therapeutic Listening Therapy - age 5-8
- P.L.A.Y. Project - age 7
- P.E.C.S. (picture exchange communication system) - age 2-8
- Social Stories - age 7-present
- Cranial Sacral Therapy - age 6-present
- Essential Oils - age 5-present
- Therapeutic Horseback Riding - age 4-present

ABA (Applied Behavioral Analysis)

We began this four-month program when Jackie was five years old. It was a wonderful learning experience. Jackie was a challenge and it seemed when other children in the program were achieving their milestones we were still battling with each goal. This program taught me how to be tough, persistent, and to not back down. Over time, each one of Jackie's goals was achieved. After the program ended, we hired an ABA therapist to come into our home and work with Jackie. It was very expensive and I felt the therapist was getting nowhere with Jackie. There were more meltdowns and chaos going on in our home for that one hour at a rate of $80 an hour (which was twelve years ago) than any means of accomplishments. Finding a therapist was difficult and pursuing that therapy fell to the wayside. Jackie is very strong-willed and some goals are challenging, but I have learned to pick my battles. Over the years, I still try to incorporate most of my goals with an ABA approach. Today, Michigan is one of the states that has fought for insurance coverage of ABA therapy. I feel early intervention with ABA therapy is key. We are currently on a waiting list for a new program to receive ABA therapy for Jackie.

Occupational Therapy/Sensory Integration Therapy

Since Jackie was first diagnosed till the present, the severity of her sensory system has always been addressed in her I.E.P.'s (Individualized Education Placement). I think this has been one of the biggest obstacles that has kept her from improving in areas. She has always worn headphones because of her sensitivity to sounds, she constantly has the need to smell things and carries around lotion or shampoo bottles to constantly distract her from the smells around her. She craves deep pressure and loves to bury herself under piles of pillows or blankets. Her need to seek sensory input is important; without it we are setting her up for sensory overload which then leads to meltdowns. Occupational therapy has helped to improve sensory desensitizing. Her therapist has been awesome over the years in exploring new ways to give her the input she needs to help calm and regulate her nervous system.

Gluten/Casein Free Diet

Many autistic children have difficulty digesting gluten and/or casein. These children have shown inflamed gastrointestinal tracts, which are particularly vulnerable to invasions by fungi especially yeast of the Candida species. Health problems known to be caused by Candida overgrowth include stomachaches, gas pains, diarrhea, headache, fatigue, and depression. Behavior problems include concentration difficulties, hyperactivity, short attention span, irritability, and aggression.

Gluten/Casein free is a healthy way of eating. It's a better way to eliminate all the processed junk that's hidden in foods today. I started Jackie on this diet when she was three years old till about the age of eight. Other ingredients that were eliminated from her diet were modified food starch and artificial colors, plus I had to watch out for ingredients that were secretly hidden in foods that contained gluten and casein. Casein is in dairy. So my plan was to substitute dairy products with soy. The problem was that Jackie's doctor wanted to also eliminate soy. Further into the diet her doctor also eliminated corn. It is important to follow this diet exactly because even minute traces of gluten and/or casein could have a drastic result on the effectiveness of this diet.

Enforcing the diet was crazy! I found myself lunging across desks at school Halloween parties blocking cookies or cupcakes from Jackie as she tried to sneak a bite. The holidays were also challenging. When the buffet table was set up at my parents' house there was food not permitted on the diet. I was like a security guard that stood close to the table making sure Jackie didn't dive for a cracker. Jackie was very limited to the food she could eat on the diet and refused to eat most of the foods that we tried. Looking back at photos I can't believe how thin she was.

Our family was more than accommodating as I tried various GFCF recipes for birthday cakes (some of which were awful!), holiday dishes, or even snacks such as gluten-free pretzels at our family events. Please keep in mind that this was fourteen years ago and GFCF items were very limited. I gave 100 percent to the diet for over four years and I really didn't see any significant improvements; however, I knew it was a much healthier way to eat. When I did eventually fade out the diet, I didn't see any regression with Jackie. I still try to incorporate some gluten/casein free food in our home because it's healthier and it eliminates processed ingredients and chemicals that so many foods contain. Every child is different and most children who have tried this diet have made significant improvements.

D.A.N. (Defeat Against Autism Now) Doctor
Glutathione Intravenously

I was on a mission to find a D.A.N. doctor as soon as Jackie was diagnosed. These are a band of doctors around the world who are on a mission to defeat autism with alternative approaches. The doctor I found was located in Wisconsin and he flew to Michigan every two months to perform glutathione intravenously (glutathione is a chemical in the body which helps us to detox toxins such as mercury, lead, arsenic, etc.). Most people are deficient in glutathione, which makes it harder for their bodies to detox unwanted chemicals.

When Jackie first started receiving the IVs at the age of four or five, she would usually vomit and become very sick and lethargic within the first twenty-four hours. I was told that it was her body trying to dump the toxins out of her system. Looking back it seemed so harsh, but again there were promising results with those people who tried glutathione intravenously so it was worth pursuing.

Our D.A.N. doctor supported a strict diet free from gluten/casein, soy, and corn. He also had Jackie on twelve to fourteen different supplements a day that I camouflaged into her juice and limited types of food she would eat. We were under our D.A.N. doctor's care for about four years. There were no significant improvements, but I often wonder if things would have been worse without trying this approach. It was a huge financial burden during those four years for us. None of these approaches were covered by insurance.

Supplements, Supplements, Supplements!

Most children who are on the spectrum are not receiving nearly the recommended amount of vitamins, minerals, and nutrients. In fact, most children are deficient in one or more minerals and vitamins. Jackie was deficient in zinc, magnesium, and calcium so we began with these supplements. These supplements came in a tasteless, odorless liquid which looked and tasted just like water. Jackie also needed help with detoxing so artichoke extract and silymarin (milk thistle), both of which support the liver, were added to her diet. I was able to camouflage these into her almond butter daily. Cod liver oil was also added and I can say that I did see an increase in eye contact after just a short time using this supplement. Other supplements such as probiotics, etc., were also added to her diet. I still use these supplements today.

A.I.T. (Auditory Integration Training) Program

Auditory Integration Therapy was developed by French otolaryngologist Guy Berard. This therapy consists of twenty, thirty-minute sessions of listening to specifically modulated music over a period of ten to twenty days. I had read the book *Sound of a Miracle*, which was about a girl with many characteristics similar to Jackie, especially the severe auditory sensitivity. The book discussed treatments of auditory listening and how it made a miraculous improvement in this person's life. I was convinced that this was the missing puzzle piece. I did research and found a doctor in the area that specialized in this form of therapy.

Jackie was seven years old when I took her on the initial consultation and they explained what was involved during therapy. Jackie would have to attend the program for approximately two weeks and during her appointment she would go into a soundproof room wearing headphones the entire time. Each day the amount of time would increase to approximately thirty minutes. The challenge was going to be keeping her in the booth and also keeping the headphones on her head the entire time.

A staff person that was working with our family at the time had agreed to take her. I had suggested this since I felt Jackie would do better without me there. Everyday staff would pick her up and commute to the office and undergo therapy. Jackie completed the program and passed with flying colors. She did great through the whole process. Unfortunately, there were no significant changes. In my opinion, this was a complete waste of time and money ($1,500) for not seeing any improvements.

Therapeutic Listening

Therapeutic Listening capitalizes on the organized rhythmical sound patterns in music to give the listener unique and controlled sensory integration. Some of the positive results are sensory modulation, increased attention, social interaction, and increased engagement in the world.

This was a successful program for Jackie. Her attention increased and she seemed more engaged. Sitting at the table through dinner was always challenging and still is. I think the sounds of silverware clanking, people chewing, and the smells of different foods send Jackie's sensory system into overload. Using therapeutic listening helped to calm Jackie and organize her nervous system. However, I was told that after receiving A.I.T., you should not use therapeutic listening. I never really found out why. I have thought about reintroducing this therapy to Jackie again.

P.L.A.Y. (Play and Language for Autistic Youngsters) Therapy

We started this intervention in the summer of 2006, when Jackie was seven years old. A therapist came to our home and trained me on different forms of P.L.A.Y. to increase engagement, turn taking, communication, etc. I loved this form of therapy and still do. It is a discreet, yet positive way to incorporate learning and accomplishing goals. The child thinks they are enjoying playtime rather than work. This allows you to teach your child without the "school room" environment. One form of P.L.A.Y. therapy that we used was pretending to be asleep. If she didn't notice that I was sleeping I would begin to snore. Then I would wait for any kind of a reaction. Once she responded by saying, "Mama, no snoring!" my response back would be with interactive play. The cycle would repeat with me pretending to sleep and snore again until I received a reaction. Her reciprocation would always be rewarded with a play activity. This therapy is still successful in increasing interaction between Jackie and me.

P.E.C.S. (Picture Exchange Communication System) Therapy

This therapy was our first stepping stone to communication. Jackie picked it up right away and used picture cards as a tool to communicate her needs and wants. We used pictures for schedules and to help make choices on different activities throughout the day. We eventually used the picture cards for social stories and schedules at school. This really helped to ease her anxiety with transitioning from one activity to the next. Plus, with pictures comes language. Today, we are able to use words for most schedules, but occasionally will use pictures. I use pictures to identify body parts or unfamiliar activities. Just a simple picture of a person with the body parts labeled has helped me to determine what hurts when Jackie is sick or doesn't feel well. The

P.E.C.S. program has been an excellent learning tool for us!

Social Stories

This has been a huge asset in transitioning and problem solving. When I was first introduced to social stories I really couldn't understand the concept and why it was necessary to write everything out. I couldn't imagine how writing things down could make such a difference, but it really does! I can tell Jackie something over and over and she may even seem engaged, but most of the time it doesn't process. With a social story, it does two things: It slows down her mind to look and read each word so she can process it slowly and effectively; and it distracts her from a particular behavior or upset and puts her attention on a visual opposed to auditory (which is over-stimulating). Social stories are our "go to" in times of trouble and transitions.

Cranial Sacral Therapy

Cranial Sacral Therapy was pioneered and developed by the osteopathic physician John Upledger. He refined Cranial Sacral Therapy (CST) after extensive scientific studies performed from 1975-1983 at Michigan State University.

I was interested in learning about CST after reading the book *My Inner Physician* by John Upledger.

Cranial Sacral Therapy is a gentle, hands-on method of evaluating and balancing the natural functioning of a physiological body system called the Cranial Sacral system. This system is comprised of membranes and cerebrospinal fluid which surround and protect the brain and spinal cord. Using a soft touch, generally no greater than five grams (or about the weight of a nickel), practitioners release restrictions in the Cranial Sacral system to improve the function of the central nervous system. It has been effective in a wide range of medical problems associated with chronic pain, illness, and sensory disorders.

I was intrigued after I learned how our bodies work and wanted to learn more about it. I decided to take an introductory course in Cranial Sacral and found it fascinating. After I completed the course, I practiced cranial on my family, but never felt confident in myself since there was still so much to learn. A friend of mine, who was a parent of a student at Jackie's school, referred me to Dennis Novelli, Cranial Sacral Practitioner. I started taking Jackie for weekly appointments. Jackie was six years old and full of energy, whirling about like a hurricane most of the time. She never sat down and was into everything. Appointments were thirty minutes, but we were lucky if we got ten minutes of cranial in. We tried putting her favorite show on the television to keep her still, but it was nearly impossible. Each week after cranial, Jackie seemed to slow down and become more focused and engaged. That small amount of improvement was worth continuing our sessions. After about one year, we decided to take a break since we were in the process of exploring new therapies.

Over the years, I have built a great friendship with Dennis. I see him regularly for cranial and occasionally I still have Jackie visit him. He is a wonderful person who has helped me through some rough times with Jackie. His positive attitude has kept me on track spiritually and emotionally. I am a huge fan of Cranial Sacral Therapy. I think this form of therapy is a positive, non-invasive form of therapy that's worth seeking.

Essential Oils

Essential oils were man's first medicine. From Chinese manuscripts and Egyptian hieroglyphics, we know that priests and physicians have been using essential oils for thousands of years.

In 2008, I took a class to learn about essential oils which was sponsored by Young Living Essential Oils. After just one class I was hooked and became a distributor. I ended up buying the starter kit and manual on all the different uses of oils. Doctor appointments were unbearable when Jackie was sick. The first thing they wanted to do was prescribe antibiotics. I was losing trust in the medical field at that time. If there was something I could use at home to help with colds and ear infections, I thought it would be worth trying. I began using oils for colds, flus, fevers, ear infections, and calming. I was impressed with the positive results. I have witnessed firsthand how essential oils have taken pain away, cleared bronchial pathways, reduced fevers, cleared sinuses, relieved upset stomachs, and more! To this day I faithfully use my oils. Essential oils and aromatherapy are a natural, safe way to help calm and relieve many symptoms.

Therapeutic Horseback Riding

I have always loved horses. They are strong animals with a serene character. It's unfortunate that when I was twelve years old I developed a severe allergy to horses. Therapeutic horseback riding is very beneficial in livening the sensory preceptors in the vestibular system. These receptors are stimulated through direction change, incline, and speed. I felt this would be a great sensory activity for Jackie to try. We started therapeutic horseback riding when she was four years old. She rode weekly for about two years. We restarted therapy again in the fall of 2014 and Jackie still continues to ride each week. This form of sensory therapy has been very positive for Jackie, plus it's fun and exciting.

Moon/Mood Connection?

Fall has always been a challenging time with behaviors for Jackie's autism. The honeymoon period from the start of a new school year is over and the anticipation of the holidays awaits. There's something about the full moon that seems to fill the air with adrenaline. From my experiences, things seem unsettled and more chaotic during a full moon.

There has been and still is an ongoing battle between scientists and researchers about the connection between full moon and lunacy (derived from the Latin word for "moon," *luna*, meaning violence, aggression, mood disorders, and anxiety). According to ancient philosophers, the moon affects human behavior and health by its gravitational pull on the body fluids. If the moon can influence tides in large bodies of water, why not water in our bodies? If the human body is made up of 60 percent water, this makes me believe that moon phases would exert an effect on human beings. Could perhaps this change in body fluids have an effect on behaviors for children on the spectrum?

Medical Marijuana

Recently, parents of autistic children, their lawyers, and supporters worked to have Michigan become the first state to support the use of medical marijuana for autism. There have been some very promising stories of families that have tried medical marijuana and saw positive results and a decrease in aggressive behaviors.

Sadly, it was denied, one reason being that there was insufficient scientific research to justify using cannabis for autism. If there is any chance of improvement, why would they deny the use of medical marijuana? It is natural and safe without all the side effects from synthetic drugs. I really wish that these individuals voting would enter into the lives of families with autistic children who are facing aggressive meltdowns! Most of them do not have a clue! If they ever witnessed just one major meltdown, they would view things much differently.

11

MEDICAL APPROACH

Though you have made me see troubles, many and bitter, you will restore my life again; from the depths of the earth you will again bring me up.

—*Psalm 71:20*

Psychiatrist, Neurologist, Psychologist, Oh My!! I made the mistake one day of calling my psychiatrist a psychologist and I was quickly corrected. A psychiatrist is required to receive a medical degree and also complete a four-year residency being trained in psychiatry. Psychiatrists can prescribe medication, whereas a psychologist can not. A Psychologists have a doctorate degree that is either a PhD or a PsyD.

During the first six years after Jackie was diagnosed, I tried every avenue imaginable to avoid medication. I have never been a fan of medicating unless it was the last resort. I always felt that behaviors were a means of communication and that it was the result of an underlying problem that needed to be addressed, rather then covered up with medication.

It was nearly two months straight that Jackie was going to bed around 10 p.m. and waking up just after midnight with severe meltdowns. Those two hours of sleep were all she required. I would sleepwalk to the coffee maker each night and make a pot of coffee for the long night ahead. I was mentally drained and exhausted.

I was quickly losing the battle with the natural approach and felt it was time to find a specialist within the medical field.

I received a call from my mother-in-law one afternoon. She called to tell me that they had recently been to a wedding and were introduced and put in touch with a neurologist, who was also the head of neurology at a well-known hospital in our area. I took down the number and called the next day for an appointment.

My husband, Jackie, and I went to our appointment and I explained in detail the increase in obsessive compulsive behaviors, severe meltdowns, and lack of sleep. I also told him that I was not a fan of medication and that this was a big step out of my comfort zone. Based on the information we gave the doctor, he thought Risperdal would be a medication that could help. He was confident and told me that if I did not see improvement within two weeks to throw the medication in the garbage.

When we left the hospital that day, I had little faith that we were going to see any positive changes. We started the medication the next day and it was almost life changing with the remarkable improvements we saw. Jackie settled down and was sleeping through the night. We were in the process of moving to a new home and new school district, which meant a new school for Jackie. The move and transition into her new school went smoothly with no problems at all. It was truly amazing!

Jackie was about eight years old when we started the Risperdal. For the next six or seven years things were manageable and remained stable. We still had challenges but the aggression was staying under control for most of the time.

A MOTHER'S PAIN

She had a glow,
Her face would show;
So happy and alive,
The tough one to survive;
Filled with energy and spirit,
Passion so alive, you could feel it;
Now it's gone, just an empty shell,
Only the sadness on her face to tell;
There's a glimpse of a smile you may occasionally see,
When her daughter responds or smiles with glee;
Although this mother still cries each night,
It's the mystery of autism that fuels her fight;
Each day leaves her emotionally drained,
Left helpless to witness her daughter's pain;
This cross she bears takes a toll,
She prays, "Dear God, please rekindle my soul."

12

THE VICIOUS CYCLE

Be strong and courageous, do not be terrified; do not be discouraged for the Lord your God will be with you wherever you go.

—Joshua 1:9

"Researchers who conducted a study at the University of Wisconsin Madison found that mothers of adolescents and adults with autism tend to have stress similar to combat soldiers…. A hormone associated with stress was extremely low, consistent with people experiencing chronic stress such as soldiers in combat," researchers reported in one of two studies published in the *Journal of Autism and Developmental Disorders.*

When Jackie is in high alert, I feel like I'm living in an abusive relationship. You never know at any given moment what is going to set her off. It may be what I say, how I look, or how I smell that will send her into a rage. When things get out of control I have learned to get out of her way. I don't try to intervene or stop her from hurting herself; instead, I get out of sight. If it meant hiding out in a closet or behind closed doors that's what I did. It wasn't worth getting hurt. It is horrifying during a bad meltdown and that's when I wish I had it on video to show doctors just exactly what Jackie and our family go through. It's during these times that I ask myself, "How can God let things get like this? And is he even with me right now?"

Problems started to surface as soon as hormones kicked in. Hormones are rough enough for girls, but then go and add all the sensory dysfunction that goes along with autism and you've got yourself a system that's out of control. We started to see aggression increase with throwing items and destroying property.

Shortly after Jackie turned fifteen years old, self-injurious behaviors skyrocketed. I believe this vicious cycle dates back to July of 2014. We went to visit our neurologist for a routine visit. The neurologist came into our room and commented on the increase in Jackie's weight. He said, "I am taking her off Risperdal." *What!* I thought to myself. *Are you kidding me!* Jackie had been on this medication for eight years. Why was he going to change something that was working?

He was advocating that medical marijuana be passed in Michigan and he said that Jackie would be a great candidate based on her behaviors and what he had seen throughout the years. In hope of medical marijuana being passed, it was necessary to wean Jackie off the Risperdal. He prescribed Xanax to be used as needed. He recommended that we begin the weaning process before the start of school. I had no idea what I was in for. That day was a life-changing moment for us.

We had planned a vacation to northern Michigan that summer at the end of July. We had rented a boathouse on the lake and also rented a boat. Friends of ours owned a cottage a few miles from there so we had planned on getting together. I had started the weaning process just prior to us leaving on vacation. I really didn't expect any drastic changes initially, plus I knew I needed to get started since the new school year was quickly approaching. Boy, was I dead wrong! Two days into our trip Jackie began going through horrible withdrawals. She would scream at the top of her lungs and violently punch her face with her fists. She looked like she was losing her mind. I was terrified. I contacted the doctor by phone and email and he explained that every child reacts differently and that this was the result of taking her off the Risperdal. He tried to reassure me that it would get better once her body adjusted.

So there we were in a beautiful vacation home, with a boat docked at the shore, and our family at our wits' end. I wanted Chris to take Cole out on the boat and do things. There was no reason why everyone should have to go through this. I stayed back with Jackie and tried to be as supportive as I could. We had planned on our staff person coming up for a couple days. She planned to stay at a hotel nearby so that she could watch Jackie as needed.

We had made plans for her to come to the house and watch Jackie for a few hours while we went to the restaurant just down the road. It was Chris's birthday and I wanted to enjoy a relaxing dinner. When we arrived at the restaurant, I was filled with anxiety and worried about if everything was going well. A glass of wine seemed to help take the edge off. I did my best to escape reality that evening so I could give my husband and son my undivided attention.

After a few hours we arrived home and found Jackie crying and our staff had a look on her face that said things didn't go too well. Jackie had gone into an upset and bit our staff's finger. This was not Jackie; she may have gotten aggressive to herself but not to others. I felt horrible. I tried to get Jackie to calm down that evening and fall asleep but her sleep pattern was all messed up. To say the least, our vacation wasn't what I had hoped for!

Within a few weeks, withdrawals seemed to be subsiding but agitation and aggression were climbing. I was giving her Xanax every four to six hours just to calm her, plus Advil because she seemed to be having headaches. September was right around the corner with the start of a new high school. I had no idea how this was going to work out. Being at home for the summer during the weaning process was a much less demanding environment.

Once high school started the behaviors began to increase and I was being called to pick up Jackie almost every day. Once Jackie figured out that aggression equals mom picking me up, the aggression and self-injurious behaviors steadily climbed. I finally ended up pulling her out of school until a plan could be put into place.

The school district held a meeting and it was determined that Jackie was not a good fit for that high school. They felt that she would benefit more by being placed in a self-contained AI (Autistic Impaired) classroom outside of our city. I wasn't pleased about moving her to a new school when the high school she was in was practically in our backyard. I did, however, want a supportive environment that had Jackie's best interests in mind. The new school that Jackie was assigned to was equipped with experienced staff that were able to handle the challenges that come with autism.

Jackie had been home with me for two months. I was witnessing horrible aggression to herself and me. There were times when she had such a crazed look in her eyes. She seemed to disappear during those moments into a dark place. I would hide out of sight, fearful of what she may do. I would tell Cole to go to his room if he heard his sister becoming upset. There was one evening when Jackie started to become very upset while taking a bath. She jumped out of the tub and lunged at me, wanting to attack. As I tried to escape out of her way she tore at my pajama bottoms tearing them to shreds. She was filled with such rage, it was terrifying to witness. Anything she could get to in her path was being thrown across the room. Glass was everywhere. As much as I wanted to escape, I was fearful to leave her alone in case she cut herself. What seemed like hours ended in minutes.

Our family was in a crisis. When there were upsets in our home it was a battlefield. The sad part is, most families are alone and left dealing with these moments. Who do they have to turn to? Police officers would probably use restraint and make matters worse or ship her to a hospital for observation. Then she would be left experiencing all of this alone with strangers who didn't understand her needs or wants. This would be a traumatic experience for all of us. Each night I would pray the rosary and beg our Blessed Mother for peace and protection to get us through another night.

During this time, Chris and I seemed to be going our separate ways within our own home. Having a conversation with him was difficult because too much talking would trigger her auditory sensitivity and cause an upset. Jackie did not want me out of her sight. I'm not sure if it was that she was becoming dependent on me being with her every minute or if she was insecure and fearful with everything she was experiencing. This was taking a toll on our family.

I was persistent with the neurologist and his nurse, begging them to do something. We tried Zoloft and Clonidine and there were no signs of improvement with either. Xanax was a short fix to relax her, but when that wore off it was almost worse. Finally, after an appointment at the neurology office and them witnessing firsthand the bite marks and bruises on her body, it was decided that Risperdal would be reintroduced. It was also recommended that I see in addition to the neurologist, a psychiatrist for Jackie.

Jackie began her new high school in January after the holiday break. The first week was horrific. She fought me every morning to get into the car. The meltdowns continued while she transitioned into school each day that first week. Eventually, she understood that mom wasn't backing down and that staying home was not an option. Each day got better as she got used to school and staff got used to Jackie. By the end of the school year, Jackie was transitioning nicely.

That following summer, Jackie began complaining about her tooth hurting. Dental exams were impossible and could only be performed while Jackie was put completely under anesthesia. I made the dental appointment and thought that while she was put under it would be a good opportunity to also have complete blood work done, since it had been years. At 5'3" and 175 pounds, it wasn't like the old days when I could lie across her and hold her while they drew blood.

On the morning of the dental exam, the dentist had prescribed medication to help her relax so that it would be easier to give her the shot which would sedate her enough to proceed with putting her IV in. The medication seemed to be working. Jackie was a little sedated and relaxed. We decided to bring her back to the room where they were going to perform the exam and once Jackie got a look at the tray holding the syringes she flipped out! Equipment was flying everywhere and the dentist, who was a large man, his dental assistant, and I wrestled to get Jackie into the chair where they injected her with the sedation to prepare her to be put under intravenously. I was relieved when the dental exam was completed and blood was drawn.

Within a week, I received a call from the psychiatrist who recommended blood work. He informed me that the blood work revealed that Jackie was lactating, which is a side effect of the Risperdal. He suggested that she be taken off of it as soon as possible before the start of school that fall. I sat silently on the other end of the phone. I was in complete shock and thought to myself, *This can not be happening to us again! Is this deja vu?* I could not believe what I was hearing.

Our psychiatrist suggested putting Jackie on Abilify (antipsychotic medication). He tried to convince me that Abilify was the new and improved drug replacement for Risperdal and that hopefully the withdrawals would not be as bad. We began slowly adding the Abilify and decreasing the Risperdal. When the Risperdal began to decrease, aggression and self-injurious behaviors began to increase.

At this point, weight gain and lactating were minor problems compared to the amount of injury she was imposing on herself throughout each day. With an increase in aggression and still no significant improvements, she was taken off the Abilify and put back on Risperdal. After her body began to adjust to the Risperdal, self-injurious behaviors and meltdowns were less intense and somewhat manageable, but still there was much room for improvement.

These were some of our worst times. *If this is God's will,* I thought to myself, *please help me!* If his will is for me to protect and love a child that requires special attention I accept that fully. It's the rage and violence I can hardly bear. I know you're not supposed to question, but I can't help but to ask why?

All medications affect people differently. It's so important for families who are affected by autism to treat each child as an individual. What works for one child may not work for another.

MOTHER MARY

Jesus? Mary? Are you there?
Please help me to overcome this fear.

These trials? Do they have to be?
My heart's so heavy and you've chosen me?

I stand and witness, so helpless with her near,
My rosary clenched in my fist, a sight I can't bear;

I beg you to shed your grace upon me,
Mother Mary, whom I love so dearly.

13
PURSUING THE PASSION

Those who hope in the Lord will renew their strength. They will soar on wings like eagles, they will run and not grow weary, they will walk and not be faint.

—Isaiah 40:31

When my world seems out of control I have to put things into control by cleaning, organizing, or doing projects. This helps me to divert my energy into something constructive. I got involved with Autism Speaks and formed a team, "Jackie's World," for their annual Walk for Autism. In 2007, I received from Autism Speaks an award for top fundraiser in the state of Michigan. Our team was also awarded top fundraising team in 2009 & 2010.

A few years later, my mother, cousin, close friend, and I flew to Washington, D.C., to join in a march to support "Green the Vaccines" hosted by Jenny

McCarthy. Jenny has been a great advocate for autism and her fight for "Green the Vaccines." Many passionate people joined together that day in support of such a great cause. It was a very uplifting experience for all of us.

When I get an idea in my head I don't stop till the mission is complete. In 2005, I decided to start an online website/store with merchandise to raise autism awareness. The store carried products for sensory integration, autism awareness merchandise, and essential oils. I enjoyed designing T-shirts, coffee mugs, water bottles, and other autism awareness merchandise. I was fortunate to have a dedicated crew consisting of my aunt, cousin, and friend, who helped to set up and work every autism event in the area. At these events, a portion of all proceeds was donated to the organization hosting the event. Our sales were successful during these events because people were pumped up. It was unfortunate that I didn't have the flexibility to travel outside of Michigan for other conferences and events. This would have helped to keep the business strong. Sadly, within a few years I closed the business. All of our unused merchandise was donated to local autism organizations.

My mission to raise awareness didn't end there. I used my profits from the business to fund an autism awareness billboard. I designed the billboard, which read "1 in 91 children are kidnapped by Autism" with a picture of Jackie on it. The billboard was up for about three months and was located on a highway north of Detroit.

I met many wonderful people while I was active in the autism community. So many touched my heart and I felt such a connection with them. It often seemed like I knew these people, yet I had never met them before. Maybe it was because we had so much in common or because we could console one another about the challenges we were facing. It was interesting to hear all the different stories; some were of success, while others were sad and heart-wrenching. When people shared a similar experience to mine, I felt the need to hug them just to let them know I cared.

After my business closed, I wanted to find work out in the community. I thought it would be rewarding to work as a para-professional with children affected by autism. I applied for a position at an elementary school in our school district. I had experience and I was passionate about helping children so it seemed perfect. I applied for the position, was interviewed, and hired. Shortly after I started, I developed a bond with each of the students. When any of the students had an upset, it was difficult because it really hit home. It wasn't any easier to watch another child go through this like I thought it would be. After just a few months, I ended up giving my notice. I felt it was just too much with everything I had going on at home. Although I only worked there a few months, it was hard to say goodbye.

14

OUR JOURNEYS

I can do all things through him who strengthens me.

—Philippians 4:13

Jackie loves Disney. I don't know a kid that doesn't like Disney. We took our first vacation by plane when Jackie was five and Cole was three and a half years old. We had a smooth commute by plane and the vacation went well. A few years later, we decided to take the plunge once again. We booked our airline tickets to Florida. On the morning of our departure, we were all very excited. Everything was going fairly smoothly. We boarded our flight and were ready for departure. The biggest challenge was keeping both children entertained for our flight. I kept them amused with movies, books, snacks, and toys. As our flight was starting to descend, Jackie began to cover her ears and became very upset, shouting, "Plane all done!" This was right after 9/11 so security was heightened. Jackie was standing up in front of her seat and because the plane had starting to descend, the flight attendant was requesting that Jackie sit down in her seat and fasten her seatbelt. The more I tried to force Jackie to get into her seat, the more her upset escalated! The flight attendant asked that I just continue to hold her on my lap while they prepared for landing. Jackie had reached a full-blown meltdown. As she screamed, scratched, and fought endlessly to break away from my arms, I continued to hold on to her as tight as I could. When we finally landed, Jackie broke away and lay between my feet on the floor of the plane sucking her thumb and holding her stuffed bunny. Not a person on that plane made a sound or eye contact. We stayed in our seats until everyone exited the plane. I could see Chris and Cole across the aisle from us. Chris and I looked at each other; neither of us said a word. We gathered our belongings and left the plane. I was filled with fright, humiliation, and sadness. I searched for the closest bathroom and escaped there to have my own meltdown.

The rest of our vacation went great. Our round-trip ticket was now a one-way ticket because there was no way any of us were getting back on a plane. We ended up renting a car for our trip home.

Spring of 2013, while our staff Brielle was still employed with us, we decided to take a road trip to Disney for spring break. All arrangements had been made. We were renting a house a few miles from Disney. Tickets for all the parks were purchased. We planned on obtaining a "Guest Assistance" pass, which would help accommodate us during long waits and crowds in lines. The Guest Assistance pass is given to individuals with disabilities. It allows the person and their party to bypass the long lines and enter the attraction through the wheelchair access entrance.

The road trip headed to Disney was surprisingly smooth. We drove from Michigan to Georgia, where we stopped at a hotel for the night, and then continued on to Orlando, Florida, the next morning. When we arrived at the rental house, we were very pleased with the location and home. We unpacked and got a good night's rest for our adventure to begin the next morning.

When we arrived at Disney World, we were all filled with excitement and anticipation, although panic began to sneak in when I observed the large crowds. Not to mention the thought of having to take a boat or train ride across the lake to get to the Disney entrance. We successfully arrived at the park entrance by boat. We entered the park and I went right to Guest Relations to inquire about our Guest Assistance pass. I was then told that they no longer have Guest Assistance passes. I inquired again with someone inside the park and received the same answer that the Guest Assistance passes were no longer available. *This is not going to sit well with Jackie,* I thought. We had always received the pass and she would expect to enter the rides through the wheelchair access.

The first ride she requested was Space Mountain. We entered into the line which was a maze, weaving back and forth. We stood at a standstill for about fifteen minutes and I could see Jackie becoming upset. I had no idea what I was going to do now that we were locked into this raveling maze filled with people. Within minutes her anxiety reached a full-blown meltdown. I was looking for a way to quickly escort Jackie out of the line but there were no openings around us. Suddenly, Chris picked her up and climbed across the ropes to the nearest emergency exit door. Brielle, Cole, and I quickly followed behind them, watching as Jackie kicked, screamed, and hit hysterically. We finally made it to the exit and Brielle and I took Jackie to the nearest bathroom. Once we got inside the bathroom, Jackie dropped to the floor, continuing to scream and hit until her nervous system could regain control. Brielle stood silently at my side. Her presence was comforting. My mind flashed to the next step of how we were going to get Jackie from this bathroom, through the park, on a boat or train, and finally to our car!

When Jackie calmed down we walked quickly through the park to the train. On the train ride back, none of us said a word. When I looked over at Cole and saw the disappointment on his face, I was consumed with guilt to think that he was cheated once again on a family vacation. When we arrived home that day, I went to relax by the pool and when I looked up, "God" was written in the sky. *Yes!* I thought. *Thank you for being with me.*

I decided to order tickets for Jackie and me to see the "Wiggles Live" at the Fox Theatre in downtown Detroit. The day of the event when we arrived downtown, the Detroit Lions were playing right across the street from the theatre where the Wiggles were playing. The streets were packed with Lions fans tailgating. The lot that I usually park in was full so I drove down to the next block where a parking garage was located.

After finally getting our car parked, taking a few flights of stairs, and walking two blocks to the theatre, Jackie was about done before we even got inside the building. I was holding my tickets ready to zip through, only to find out that we had to go through a metal detector and purse check. We managed to make it through with no problems. We headed to our seats, which I chose in the last row on the aisle, close to the exit, for an easy escape if necessary.

The theatre was packed with kids screaming, singing, throwing tantrums, shouting, jumping. I was overloaded so I could only imagine what Jackie was going through. When I looked over, she seemed to be enjoying the show. It was after about fifteen minutes when

I could hear her getting louder and becoming upset as she began hitting her legs. This was our cue to leave. I was able to convince her to come with me to the lobby to look at T-shirts. As we entered the lobby her behaviors were escalating. She kept requesting to go to the bathroom, which is where we have taught her to go during an upset in public. As much as I tried to stay calm, all I kept picturing in my mind was a meltdown, out of control with children around, and how I was going to get her from the theatre to the car on my own. We managed to get to the restroom safely. After Jackie seemed to calm, I escorted her up the stairs to leave the building. A young mom and her daughter, who was around two years old, were in front of us on the stairs. Jackie was trailing close behind them, when the mom in front of us turned around and shouted, "Do you mind!!" I responded, "I'm sorry, my daughter has special needs." Her response was, "Well, doesn't she see us here?" My reply was, "Why don't you try being a little more understanding!" It ended there and Jackie and I left the building.

Children and adults with autism face challenges every minute of every day. I expect people to be more understanding and give them a break. I know what my daughter goes through and I can't help but be defensive. If people don't understand and are ignorant to what autism really is, then it's time they start to educate themselves.

15

SIBLINGS

And the child grew and became strong; he was filled with wisdom, and the grace of God was on him.

—Luke 2:40

Children on the spectrum range from mild to severe, which have different effects on each family. I have always said that what seems better or easier for one family may not be true. Having a child who is nonverbal is very frustrating, yet a child who is verbal and able to communicate their frustrations is just as complicated because there are times when helping them is out of your control. I guess the same is true for siblings. If you have a sibling on the spectrum who is very introverted and nonverbal, you try to work at communicating or connecting. On the other hand, if your sibling is extremely sensitive to noise and is aggressive you learn to stay out of their way and shy away from any interaction. When you witness your sibling during violent meltdowns or attacking others, you hold resentment against them.

This is all normal and I get it, but what breaks my heart is when our son opens up and tells me how unfair it is and asks why God did this to him. I don't have an explanation, but I tell him that God must think he's pretty important to handle this big of a job and that one day he will be rewarded for all his patience and courage.

Cole entered this world determined. On the day he was born I expected a long labor, but within forty-five minutes he was delivered. His determination has grown with him over the years. He started playing baseball at the young age of six and started football when he was eight. His determination and hard work have helped him achieve goals and excel in sports. Cole attends a Catholic high school where he receives a great education and is active in their sports program. When Cole puts his mind and heart into something, he can achieve anything. He hopes to one day play Division 1 college baseball.

Cole has always avoided having his friends come to our house in fear that his sister will act out. Teenagers are embarrassed about everything so when you add the exposure of a sibling with special needs and behaviors, your house is completely out of the question. Luckily, he has built friendships with some amazing boys who have reassured him that they are okay with Jackie's autism and that they understand. It wasn't till recently that his friends started coming over and staying the night at our house. When he has his friends over, they usually stay in another part of the house and if there is an upset I'll usually tell Cole and give him a heads-up. Little by little Cole seems to be letting his guard down.

I don't think Cole realizes how much I love him. Although he thinks he takes the backseat most of the time, it's not intentional. Jackie requires most of my attention, most of the time. I wish he would understand that this is not by choice. It seems even harder now that he's a teenager. It's easy for him to use these tools against me and bring up how everything I do revolves around his sister. I pray that one day he will understand that there was never any less love for him. I was only doing what I needed to do at the time. Little does he know, he is my rock. If it wasn't for Cole I would probably find reasons to not get out of bed some days. He is my son, whom I love with all my heart and am so very proud of. What Cole doesn't realize is that being a witness to his sister's challenges every day is shaping his character. These challenges he witnesses will help him build compassion, unconditional love, and a stronger faith.

16

GROWING UP

For I know the plans I have for you, declares the Lord, plans to prosper you and not harm you, plans to give you hope and a future.

—Jeremiah 29:11

It's hard to believe that Jackie is seventeen years old. School meetings, which are held with the best interests of the student in mind, can be mentally draining to the parents. You feel alone at a table surrounded with teachers, social workers, therapists, and the principal. Often, some are quick to judge and see me as a neurotic mom. Let me be frank: "Unless you have walked in my shoes for as long as I have, please keep an open mind and don't be so quick to judge." Fortunately, I've been blessed with wonderful support from our school system. They have listened to what I've had to say and have taken my suggestions. I have heard stories where it's unfortunate when topics become heated and emotions take over.

Every year I fill out paperwork for Jackie's IEP (Individualized Education Plan). Some of the questions listed are: please describe your child, what activities do they enjoy, please list their strengths and their weaknesses. Jackie needs structure and schedules to follow. It is difficult during school breaks trying to fill activities throughout the day to keep her busy. When a day is left open with nothing to do, obsessive behaviors surface. For Jackie, an idle mind is the devil's workshop.

My description of Jackie is that she is a beautiful young lady with long wavy hair the color of auburn with natural golden highlights. She has big brown eyes that can look straight into your soul. She has an endless memory that captures every detail of every event. She swims like a mermaid and is addicted to the scent of suntan lotion. She loves music, singing, and dancing. She loves animals and has been visiting the zoo and/or farm every weekend since she was a toddler.

Jackie is extremely bright. She is honest and pure. She doesn't lie, gossip, cheat, or steal. Her only weakness is that she is locked in a world of her own often unable to cope with her outside surroundings. This leads to uncontrollable meltdowns.

Jackie will finish her post–high school program when she is twenty-six years old. I pray every day that in time her behaviors will become stable so that she can work in the community. I envision Jackie working with animals. She seems to have a connection with them. Animals calm her and bring a smile to her face. Working on a farm with horses would be an excellent job opportunity.

Death is a difficult subject. I have a difficult time trying to explain this to Jackie. When someone close to us passes away, I'm not sure how I will explain why they left or where they went. A few years ago, our Golden Retriever of 10 years, Yankee, passed away. When Jackie realized he was gone she would repeat, "No barking, Yankee!", which was her way of inquiring about Yankee's whereabouts. I decided to tell her that Yankee left us and went up into the sky where the stars are. I knew this would be left with no open end, since our galaxy was a destination too far away for me to take her to. Our galaxy of endless stars almost reminds me of heaven.

So what happens when Chris and I pass away? This is one of my biggest fears. Who will step in and look after Jackie? I know Cole will always be there for his sister, especially to oversee and make sure she is well taken care of, but he needs freedom to build his own life. Who will protect her, and be her voice? I am hoping that we will find a compassionate person to grow with our family. Someone who will become an extended part of our family to help with Jackie. I have to believe that we can prepare as much as possible, but God will finalize the details.

17

STAYING AFLOAT

For it is by Grace you have been saved, through Faith and this not from yourselves, it is the Gift of God.

—Ephesians 2:8

My generation grew up on *The Brady Bunch*. I would race home from school to watch the next episode each day. I didn't care if it was the twentieth rerun, I couldn't get enough. I idolized that family! As I think back, *The Brady Bunch* was as far from reality as you could get. Maybe that's why I loved it so much. Back then, I never imagined a world where the chances of having a child with autism would be 1 in 83. In 2001, our daughter became a number in that statistic. Instead of running, I embraced it. However, I often ask why God gave me this job. Clearly, I'm not what seems to be the perfect candidate. I'm emotional,

I can be impatient, and I'm a perfectionist. These characteristics don't seem fit for the mom of a child with autism.

I know there are plenty of people who would choose to institutionalize their child and then carry on with their lives. I can't imagine this. Jackie is my flesh and blood. I see all the beautiful gifts inside her rather than just the dark side of autism.

As our children grow and become adults, I want to enjoy time with my husband and reap the benefits of retirement. I want freedom to travel and do things together. Having someone I can trust to watch over Jackie is what I hope for. A time may come when I have to surrender and look at other options. When and if that happens, I pray that my faith will confirm in my heart the right decision to make.

"Coincidences are when God remains anonymous..." I thank God for the coincidences in my life when my faith was confirmed. It was years ago when a Miraculous Medal of the Blessed Mother appeared on a sofa table in our living room out of nowhere. It was very old and tarnished and I had never seen it before. It's still a mystery how that medal got there. I believe it was some kind of a sign to pray to the Blessed Mother. On days when my frustrations and tiredness get the best of me, I imagine me on my knees, emptying out of my arms all my troubles at the feet of the Blessed Mother. Relying on faith that things will get better.

While we were short staffed, I had fallen out of my routine of attending mass on Sundays. I decided to start going in the mornings during the week. The first day I arrived at the daily mass, the saint for the day appeared on the screen in front of the church. Saint Hilary of Poitiers was listed. This saint represents children with disabilities. I feel this was a sign letting me know that mass was where I needed to be that day.

As I continue my life's journey, I will still hit road-blocks along the way, but I will always remember these five to survive:

- Count my blessings
- Rely on God for guidance
- Practice faith to keep strong
- Hold on to hope for reasons to strive
- Learn more about autism to keep my passion alive

THE MESSAGE

First words, then silence, then it wasn't long,
till I knew there was something terribly wrong;
No longer a response when I would call,
our child locked outside an invisible wall;
Drowning my pillow with tears on my bed,
a voice softly spoke inside my head;
I sent you this angel, you need to be strong,
I'm here right beside you and have been all along;
It's not a mistake that I have chosen you,
there are many parents on this journey too;
Love this child and never give up hope,
your faith and prayers will help you cope;
A hidden message these children are here to bring,
their reward awaits them at the gates where angels sing;
My tears went dry, I had no need to weep,
I then closed my eyes and fell fast asleep.

ACKNOWLEDGMENTS

All my love and thanks to:

My husband, who has accompanied me on our runaway train even when it's derailed. My son, and my rock, whom God has greatly blessed me with. "You keep me going, when the going gets tough". My mom and best friend, who has always been there, especially to listen. My dad, whom I inherited my strong will from. My grandparents, who have instilled morals and values in me. My family and friends, who have been there for love and support. My daughter, Jackie, whom God has given me to love, protect, and most of all learn from.

ABOUT CYNDI

The diagnosis of autism can be devastating. Fifteen years ago when her daughter was diagnosed with autism, Cyndi Sibley, a devoted mother of two and wife, became an activist in the autism community. Her mission was to erase this label from her daughter's life. Countless interventions, therapies, and a strong determination kept her searching for a cure. Throughout the many challenges she has relied on her faith to maintain a positive outlook. Experience a glimpse of her journey and be enlightened on the power of faith.

CPSIA information can be obtained at www.ICGtesting.com
Printed in the USA
BVOW08s2041050916
461196BV00001B/5/P

9 781367 913608